Cooking with Justin

Cooking with Justin

Recipes for Kids (and Parents) by the World's Youngest Chef

Justin Miller

Andrews and McMeel
A Universal Press Syndicate Company
Kansas City

Designed by Randall Blair Design.

Library of Congress Cataloging-in-Publication Data

Miller, Justin, 1990-
    Cooking with Justin : recipes for kids (and parents) by the world's youngest chef / by Justin Miller.
        p. cm
    Summary: The author presents some of his favorite recipes and describes how he became a chef at the age of five.
        ISBN 0-8362-2577-5 (pbk.)
        1. Cookery. {1. Cookery. 2. Children's writings.}
TX652.5.M54 1997
641.5—dc21   96-37199
                                                    CIP
                                                    AC

Contents

Recipes

Contents

indicates degree of difficulty.
= piece of cake!
= almost easy as pie
= holy mackerel!

Acknowledgments

I would like to thank a lot of people who have supported me, taught me, and helped show me the proper way to be a good cook. My mom, who always has patience and says, "If you make a mess, be sure to clean it up." My dad, who used to hold me when I was too little to see into the pots and pans. My nannis, Betty and Tina, who showed me some different ways to do things. My pappaps, Joe and Wally, for their support, and a whole list of media people who helped me to have this dream come true:

The staffs of the *Late Show with David Letterman, Donahue, Good Morning America*, Gloria Hilliard and CNN, *Talk Soup*, Chris, Justin, and *Inside Edition*, Leeza Gibbons, *Mister Rogers' Neighborhood*, and all of my friends at the *Mike & Maty Show*, which was taped in Hollywood, California. I miss you all.

In addition, I have appeared on KDKA television in Pittsburgh, my home town, lots of times with Jon Burnett and Larry Richert, WTAE-TV with Liz Miles, a show called the *Morning Exchange* in Cleveland, Ohio, and nationally syndicated radio shows such as *After Midnite* with Blair Garner.

Many newspaper reporters have kept the people informed about what I've been doing. Thanks to Barbara Vancheri and the *Pittsburgh Post Gazette*, Debbie Galle, Marsha Keefer, Rachael, and others, and the *Beaver County Times*, the *Tribune Review*, Ione Morgan and the *News*, and Michelle Wong and the *Cleveland Plain Dealer*. The Associated Press ran a story, which was published in

Acknowledgments

newspapers all over the country.

At Pittsburgh radio station WDSY, a special thanks to Joe Armao, general manager, for letting my dad have the time off so he could travel with me, and to the entire staff for their support. Jimmy Roach, Ellen Gamble, and Monty helped keep the listeners up to date with daily phone interviews while we were in New York and Hollywood. Barry Beck of WVTY, Mike Romigh of KDKA, Sean McDowell, WDVE, Carl Anderson, and Bill Cameron of WWKS, Frank Iorio and John Nuzzo, WBVP, and a special thanks to our backyard radio station WMBA, especially to Brad Richards, for all the air time and support.

Although the media has been fantastic, a special heartfelt thanks to all the people who kept calling the radio and television stations, and the newspapers asking what was next and giving me support. There is one other person that I would like to thank: Doug Kaleugher. He is my dad's friend and boss at Med-Fast Pharmacy.

And lastly, three very special thank yous—first to my book agent, Frank Weimann at The Literary Group, who knew he would find a publisher out there if he knocked on enough doors; to the great folks on the other side of that door, Nora Donaghy, Jake Morrissey, Cynthia Borg, and more at Andrews and McMeel; and last but not least, my manager and friend, Phil Lobel, who from the day I met him backstage at the *Late Show with David Letterman* has never stopped believing.

I am extremely grateful that I have had this opportunity, mainly because a lot of people have told my mom and dad that they have always been afraid of letting their children in the kitchen while they are cooking. Since seeing me on TV, more and more people can see that as long as grown-ups supervise kids and teach them that the kitchen and appliances are not a playground, cooking can be a very fun and worthwhile experience for both parents and kids. Remember, always emphasize safety first and just have fun!

Chef Justin

Introduction

Hi! My name is Justin Miller, and welcome to my first cookbook. I was born January 10, 1990, and ever since I can remember I've wanted to be a chef. The first question people ask me is "How did you get started cooking?" Well, it all started when I began to crawl. I found out that I could go into the kitchen cupboards and pull out the pots and pans.

Mommy and Daddy decided since I liked playing in the kitchen so much they would put all of the dangerous stuff out of reach and let me play with the pots, pans, and utensils that wouldn't hurt me. Soon, I was in my high chair watching Mommy cook dinner. Daddy would even hold me sometimes so I could get a closer look. I watched her cook every day. Mommy would talk to me and tell me what ingredients she was putting into the pots and pans and why.

When I was in the kitchen I loved to watch things get mixed up. My favorite utensil is the whisk, and I really like the blender, juicer, milk shake maker, and food processor. One day, when I was about eighteen months old, Mommy was making pigs in a blanket. Some people call them cabbage rolls. So I was sitting in my high chair, and Mommy put a big bowl of stuff and a cabbage leaf in front of me. I guess she needed some help, so I grabbed some of the mix in the bowl, put it on the cabbage leaf, and rolled it up like she did. I hand-ed it to Mommy, and she started laughing and called Daddy into the kitchen. She said, "Watch this—I don't believe it." She gave me another cabbage leaf, and I did it again. Mommy and Daddy both seemed really excited. I don't see what the big deal was. I've been in the kitchen ever since I could crawl!

As I got bigger, Mommy and Daddy would let me do more in the kitchen. I made peanut butter and jelly sandwiches, helped Mommy and my two grand-mas with cooking and baking, and had lots of fun.

When I was two, Santa Claus brought me a little toy kitchen that I had seen on TV. Soon I was chopping with plastic utensils, had my very own whisk, a toy blender, mixer, pots and pans, and I could cook any time I wanted to. Mom would give me some lettuce, carrots, spices, and I made up some of my own recipes. At first some of them weren't too good, but like anything, it takes time to get it right. I still helped out in the real kitchen, too.

Besides cooking in the kitchen, I also watched cooking shows on TV. Graham Kerr was my favorite chef, and I would watch him twice a day. He is very funny and a very good chef. I also liked Wolfgang Puck.

One day when I was four, we were watching Graham Kerr's program and Dad suggested he videotape me cooking and send it to Graham Kerr. I was so excited. I got all dressed up, put on a pair of suspenders and said I wanted it to be like a TV show. I came running into my kitchen, and Mommy gave me real food and helped me remember how to make a vegetable pot pie. I cooked it up, took it to the dining room, and showed how many calories and fat were in the dish. That's what Mr. Kerr does. Daddy sent the tape to Mr. Kerr. Pretty soon I received a letter and an autographed picture from him. He said in the letter that I do very well chopping and cutting with a plastic knife—not that easy to do. I was so excited I told Dad to put the letter in a frame.

The next thing I knew, Mom and Dad asked me if I wanted to cook for the *Beaver County Times*, a local newspaper. It was my chance to cook in a real kitchen, so I said sure. When they came, there was a lady, Debbie Galle, with a tape recorder, tablet, and pen, and a man, Pete Sabella, with a camera and lights. I had just turned five. We talked and talked while I made chicken crescent roll-ups, zucchini rings, and mini-cheesecakes, with some help around the stove from my mom. Dad videotaped me cooking. I was all dressed up and did just about everything myself.

In a couple weeks, the paper came out and there were three color pictures of me, the three recipes that I cooked, and a story about my autographed picture from Mr. Kerr and how I could cook. They called me "chef boy-o-boy" and everyone started calling me Chef Justin. Dad took the newspaper and a tape he made with Charles Vandergrift at Creative Images Video and said he was sending it to some guy on TV named David Letterman. I remember everyone saying Daddy was crazy. The next week a nice lady from the show named Leigh Ann called and talked to Dad and then to me for about a half hour. We talked about cooking, my friends, preschool, and all kinds of cool stuff. She was very nice. Mom and Dad asked me if I would like to be on television. I told them I would do it if I could cook.

Introduction

After about three or four weeks of talking to people from the *Late Show with David Letterman*, Mom and Dad said we were going to fly in a jet to New York and asked if I wanted to make my favorite recipe, mini-cheesecakes, on TV. They didn't have to ask twice!

On April 25, 1995, we flew to New York, and stayed in this big hotel with a revolving door, the Rihga Royal. It was very cool. So was the big limo that took us there from the airport. The next morning we got up early, and a limo took us to the *Late Show*. We went upstairs and met Leigh Ann Gibson, Mary Collins, and Sarah Langford, these ladies I had talked to on the phone. They were all very nice, but Mary was my favorite. She made me laugh and laugh. They told me we were going to practice making my mini-cheesecakes down in the studio and to put my jacket on because it was very cold. They said Dave likes it that way.

When we went downstairs I was showing Mary how to make the recipe when a man named David Copperfield came in. Mary said we were going to go to the green room while he practiced an illusion that he was doing on the show that night. We went into the green room, and do you know what? There isn't even anything green in it. Except a couple plants. Anyway, there was this man named Phil Lobel in there talking to all these people from CBS about a David Copperfield show that was going to be on the next Monday. I just started telling Mary knock-knock jokes and played a little bit. Mom and Dad were there, too. I don't go anywhere without them, or my stuffed friend, Mr. Blue, who stayed at the hotel.

Pretty soon I went out to the stage with Mary again and I showed her how to make mini-cheesecakes. When we were finished, Leigh Ann took us up to my dressing room. Mary had some things to do and said she would see me later. David Copperfield had a dressing room and so did a musician named David Sanborn. There was somebody else on the show, too, but she was in a downstairs dressing room. Her name was Kathie Lee Gifford, and she was on first. After a while my dad came in and asked if I would like to take a picture with David Copperfield, so I said sure. We took the picture, and I asked my dad if I could take a picture with Phil Lobel. Dad said yes. I really liked Phil. He seemed like a pretty nice guy, and he made me laugh. Before David Copperfield went on stage, Phil came in and asked my parents if they would like me to be in commercials or movies. He said he would like to be my manager, and he gave them a card. After Phil left, Mom and Dad asked Leigh Ann if he was serious. She had a funny look on her face and

Me and my parents with David Letterman

said, "Yes, he was." She said she never saw that happen before.

Soon, I was in the green room. Then they took me to another room where they combed my hair, but said I didn't need very much makeup. There were a lot of bright lights and mirrors in there. Then it was back to the green room,

Introduction

where everyone was watching David Copperfield put a woman in a box and move her around in pieces. I asked how he did that and no one would tell me. After he was done Mary came in and said that there were only two minutes left because the segment went a little long. I could either go on now for two minutes or we could stay in the Rihga Royal another night, borrow their limo, and I could come back tomorrow and have four minutes. Mom and Dad asked me what I wanted to do. I really liked that revolving door, so I said let's stay and come back tomorrow. We did.

We arrived at the *Late Show* in a stretch limo at about one o'clock in the afternoon. Mary wanted to rehearse some more so we made some mini-cheese-cakes and she told me some things that Dave might say to me on stage. Mom and Dad asked who was on the show that night. Leigh Ann said Michael J. Fox and Anita Baker. She said since I was bumped the night before, I would go on second, after Michael J. Fox.

At about 3:30, we went to my dressing room upstairs and Leigh Ann said I had to go to makeup. She took me down and I met Michael J. Fox, who was in makeup, too. He was very nice.

We went to the green room after that, and they said they were going to bring in the audience; it was about 4:30. There were a lot of people in the green room, a couple of guys named Sirijul and Mujibar, and a bunch of clowns. They were from Ringling Brothers and Barnum and Bailey Circus. They were all very nice and they tried to teach me to balance a bowling pin and to juggle. I threw these rings up in the air, but I couldn't catch them because they flew across the room.

That was the end of my juggling lesson. Then someone came in and said they had to close the door for a couple of minutes because Michael J. Fox was going on stage. The television was on and Dave had just said Michael was coming up next. Soon the door opened and they told me I had to get miked. They put this little box on the back of my belt and ran this wire up through my sweater and clipped this tiny microphone to my shirt. They said I would be going on stage in a couple of minutes. I asked where Mom and Dad would be and Mary told me they would be watching in the green room and would meet me right after I cooked. They said that would be okay, so I thought it was okay, too.

Before I was introduced, Mary told me not to worry about the loud music because Paul Shaffer was going to play softly on the piano. Pretty soon Dave said something like, "And now, ladies and gentlemen, you're in for a real treat." He went over to the stove and put his hand on the burner and said, "Is this thing on?" (He knew it was not.) Then he screamed and started shaking his hand like he was burned. He's a silly guy. He wasn't burned, he was just pretending. Everyone laughed. Then Dave said, "We have the world's only chef who's not allowed to touch a stove without adult supervision. Ladies and gentlemen, five-year old Justin Miller. Justin?" When he said that, someone told me to go ahead out on stage to Dave. I went running out full blast, just like on my video that I made for Graham Kerr.

We never did get around to making mini-cheesecakes. We talked, tossed cookies into the audience, and Dave put an egg on a spoon and flung it into the band. When our time was up, Dave gave me a brand-new blender that we were going to use to make the mini-cheesecakes. I had a present for him, too, and gave it to him later. Dave asked me if I would like to stay on stage with him while Anita Baker sang her song. I really liked Dave, so I said sure. He said he had to ask my mom and dad first, though, to make sure it was okay. Mary left for a minute and came back and said it was okay for me to stay on stage. We

had fun talking about a flying rat Dave had on some wires, and then Anita Baker came out and sang a song. I really liked the song she sang. We were going to give her some of the cheesecakes I made before the show, but when Dave went to hand them to me, they accidentally dropped on the floor.

When the show was over we took pictures on the set and I remembered I had a gift for Dave—a piece of bubble gum that I had brought for him all the way from Pittsburgh. I like bubble gum and wanted to give Dave something

I met my manager, Phil Lobel, backstage at the *Late Show with David Letterman.*

good. Dave came to a downstairs room where there were a lot of pictures on the wall. I didn't really know anybody up there, but my mom and dad did. There was some guy named Ed Sullivan with a little mouse named Topo-Gigio. He was cute. Mom and Dad said the theater we were in was named after Ed Sullivan because he did a show there before Mr. Letterman. There were other pictures, too, of some guys called The Beatles, The Stones, The

Doors, and Elvis Presley. Leigh Ann told my mom and dad that I was on the very same stage where all these people got their big break.

Soon Dave came in. A lady was with him carrying a bag with some T-shirts and sponges. Dave had an autographed football and he tossed it to me and said, "Here, Justin, here's a present for you." "Cool, thank you," I said. Dave gave the bag to my parents and said, "Mr. and Mrs. Miller, you have a wonderful little boy there." I tossed him the football and said, "Oh yeah, and I have something for you, too. I brought it all the way from Pittsburgh. I hope you like it." I gave him the bubble gum and he smiled and said he liked it very much. We took a picture with him, talked for a few minutes and he had to go. Dave is a very nice man. He's very funny. I really hope I get to see him again sometime.

The Local Media

When we got home it was very late, and Mom and Dad said we had to go to sleep because I was going to be on KDKA-TV with Jon Burnett and Brenda Waters to tell them about being on the *Late Show*. I was very tired, but it's fun being on TV. We arrived at KDKA at around 6:15 A.M. I waited in the green room until they told me to come out to the set at around 6:50. They were very nice and offered us breakfast. When we went on to the set, I took my football and blender, to show Jon and Brenda. They thought they were really cool. During a commercial, Jon and I tossed the football back and forth. After the television interview, we walked across to the radio station where Dad works. It's called WDSY or Y–108. There were a couple of guys there who wanted me to talk on their show, Jimmy Roach and Monty. They asked me all about Dave. Boy, people sure do ask a lot of questions about that guy. After we talked, Jimmy Roach said that since I only got a couple hours of sleep that I should go home and "go to bed." I started laughing and said, "No, you go home and go to bed." We hollered that back and forth a few times and Monty said he had to step in and break it up because it was getting ugly. They are very funny guys, and I'll bet people listening thought we were crazy, but we were just having fun.

Donahue

For a couple of days, a lot of people called to say they had seen me on the *Late Show with David Letterman*. Some were people we knew and some were not. I remember Mom and Dad saying they got a phone call from someone named Phil Donahue who asked if I would like to go back to New York and make my mini-cheesecakes on his show. I asked if we would get to stay at the Rihga Royal, because I really liked that revolving door. They didn't know where we would stay, but told me it would probably be a nice hotel, so I said okay. Soon we were on a jet and going back to New York. Did I tell you our luggage got lost? Both times? Luckily, we got it back in time for the shows.

When we got to the studios there were a lot of kids there. The show was about amazing kids. All the kids were nice. There was one who was a computer whiz, a college graduate at the age of twelve, one who helped his mother have a baby, and one kid who wrote to the governor to get a pardon to get out of trouble with his parents. They took us all into the green room—nothing green in there, either, and one by one took us to makeup.

I was hoping I would have a chance to rehearse, but since there were so many people on the show, I didn't. I was on first. They had a little counter set up with all of the ingredients on it and told me to stand there until Phil Donahue came out. So I did. He came out and talked to the audience for a couple of minutes, told them about the show and then came over to me and said, "Justin, we're on." I looked at him and said, "Uh-huh." I was

Me and my dad with Phil Donahue

explaining to him how to make the mini-cheesecakes, and when it came time to add the eggs, I asked if he would put them in the blender for me. I told him I wasn't too good at cracking eggs because I usually get the shell in. He laughed and said, "To tell you the truth, so do I." Phil took one egg and said, "I'll tell you what. I'll do one and then you crack the rest. You've got to learn sometime, right?" I said, "Right." He took the egg in one hand and do you know what? He cracked it with only one hand! He said, "Okay, now your turn." I took an egg, cracked it, and guess what? No shell. I was so happy. The audience must have been, too, because they started clapping and cheering. After the *Donahue* show we flew back on a propeller plane. It took longer to get home and it was a bumpy ride. They called it turbulence. I didn't like the turbulence too much, but in a way it was kind of fun getting bounced around.

Hollywood

Mom and Dad had been talking with Mr. Lobel about being my manager and Phil invited us to Hollywood. We flew out for a week in June 1995. I got to cook at the Roosevelt Hotel, where we stayed, with Wolfgang Puck at his restaurant, Spago, for David Hasselhoff's wife and daughter, Pamela and Taylor, and at the Hard Rock Cafe. There were cameras from CNN that followed me around, a reporter named Gloria Hilliard, and a whole bunch of people called paparazzi taking pictures. I was on the news on television, in the *Los Angeles Times*, and a magazine type of paper called *Variety*. A man named Army Archerd said in his column that I was in town cooking.

Wolfgang Puck and I cooked for Pamela and Taylor Hasselhoff

Phil also arranged for us to go to Disneyland. I did another TV show called *Mike & Maty*. It was a lot of fun. I got to cook with co-host Michael Burger, a comic. He was very funny, too. I became really good friends with Mike and Maty Monfort.

Boy, what a great week. Mom and Dad said that Phil was going to be my manager and that he had represented such people as David Copperfield, Brad Pitt, George Michael, Billy Joel, and other celebrities. I didn't really know what they meant, but I knew I would get to see Phil again and that made me happy. Phil said I was going to be doing TV shows, flying to New York and Hollywood, and that I would get to write my very own cookbook.

Good Morning America

Phil called in July and asked if I would like to be on *Good Morning America* to cook. If I can cook, I will go, so I said sure. In August, we were off to New York. While getting ready for bed at the hotel, I noticed that Mr. Blue was nowhere to be found. I had been carrying him at the airport while Dad was talking to the people about our lost luggage again. Dad called the airport. For some reason our luggage wanted to go to Philadelphia instead of New York. Anyway, Dad asked this lady if there was a blue stuffed animal sitting around looking lonely. Several hours had passed since we were there, and we were afraid someone picked him up. After a few minutes she came back on the phone and said she had found Mr. Blue and that she would send him over with our luggage when it arrived. My Nanni Betty gave me Mr. Blue when I was born. He's my best friend.

Our luggage came and so did Mr. Blue. It was about 10:30 P.M. when he got to the hotel, and he was very tired.

The next morning we had to get up very early, around 5:30, to take showers

Introduction

and eat breakfast. A limo came to take me to the studio so I could cook live with Joan Lunden and Charles Gibson. They were very nice and had this great big fish tank on their set. I took a picture of it.

While waiting to do my segment on *Good Morning America*, one of the stage-hands asked if we would like a tour of the studio. It was really big. He showed us where world news was done and asked if I would like to have a picture taken sitting in Morton Dean's chair, behind the news desk. Mom and Dad thought that would be a great idea and asked me to sit behind the desk.

I decided I'd rather play and said no and began laughing. Right about then Mr. Dean came into the studio and asked me to sit behind the desk so that we could take a picture. I said, "No, and you can't make me." Morton said, "We'll see about that," and started to take his suit jacket off. I started laughing and running around the room. Morton started the chase. He finally caught me and put me behind his desk while I was laughing my head off. Dad snapped the picture, and Morton told me I could get up now. I started laughing again and said, "No. I want to stay here while you do the news." I didn't, but Mom and Dad said, "Where is the video camera when you really need one?"

I got to go to the kitchen and make some mini-cheesecakes and zucchini rings with one of the producers and some chefs who were there. It was fun, and one of the cooks tried to teach me to flip the zucchinis without using a flipper. He just kind of tossed them in the air. The pan was a little bit too big for me to do it, though.

Soon it was time to show Joan and Charles how to make Mrs. Zigerell's zuc-

14

Zucchini Rings. I really had a lot of fun. Joan and Charles tried the zucchini and had some of the mini-cheesecakes that I had made a little bit earlier. The stage hands had some, too. Everyone said they really liked them. I guess they did because they all got eaten. I don't know if Morton Dean got any or not, but I got to take some to the crew, and they gave me some computer pictures of Joan, Charles, and me right off the TV. I didn't know they could do that. They gave me one of the fish tank, too. I really like that fish tank.

Some people want to know how I can go to school and be on TV. Well, while I was in preschool, I would just make up the work when I came home. I went only three days a week, so it wasn't so bad. Plus

Me with Spencer Christian, Joan Lunden, and my mom and dad

my teachers didn't mind me going to New York or Hollywood.

When I started kindergarten, it was a little different. Whenever I would go to Hollywood or New York to do a show, they would have a tutor on the set and we would go over my work in my dressing room. Actually, this was a good thing because in September, right when school was starting, I went to

Introduction

Hollywood for six weeks. I did my lessons and had new ones mailed to me so I could keep up. It was really nice of Mrs. Persi and the school to do that for me. Mom and Dad said I have to keep up with my schoolwork or I couldn't cook on television anymore.

While I was in Hollywood, I started doing the *Mike & Maty Show* on a regular basis. It was a lot of fun. I signed with an agency, and they said maybe I could do movies or commercials. I only want to do them if I get to cook or movies if David Letterman or Michael Burger is in them, too.

Michael Burger and I became good friends during my trips to Hollywood.

Phil got us tickets to go to Disneyland, Knotts Berry Farms, and Universal Studios. They were all a lot of fun. My Nanni Tina came with us to California for a vacation and we took her to see the Crystal Cathedral, which is beautiful.

When it was time to go back home, I was sad because we had made many new friends. Phil said not to worry because I would get to see them all again really soon. He was right, too. Because just about five weeks later, I got to go back out to Hollywood to tape some more *Mike & Maty* shows.

In May of 1996, I went out to Hollywood to be on *Leeza*, and I showed Mister Rogers how to make turtle sandwiches on his show *Mister Rogers'*

Neighborhood. That show is filmed in Pittsburgh. I really liked doing Mister Rogers because I watch him all the time. He is very nice and he introduced me to Daniel the tiger. I scratched his stripe, because it is always itchy. I met the rest of the people in the village, too.

See, it just goes to show what you can do. Even if you're only five years old!

I showed Mister Rogers how to make turtle sandwiches on *Mister Rogers' Neighborhood.*

Safety Tips
from My Mom and Dad

When Justin began his endeavor into the culinary world, Linda and I were very concerned about safety. One day we got down on the floor to his level, and we were surprised at what we found. Our kitchen cupboards were very easy to open, and what do you think was inside? Cans of tomato paste, cans of soup, cans, cans, cans! We opened the cupboard under the sink and there was dish soap, lemon-scented furniture polish, rags to wipe the furniture polish with, and floor cleaner, but at least it was pine-scented. Naturally, from Justin's point of view the counter, the table, and the stove seemed rather inviting. We checked out the upper cabinets that were out of our son's reach and what do you suppose we found there? Potato chips, cookies, pretzels, peanuts, bags of noodles . . . what's wrong with this picture? We have all the safe items where he can't reach, and cans that are capable of crunching his little toes, furniture polish, and dish soap where they are all accessible to him. Needless to say, we made many changes. The cans went into the upper cabinets, the cleaners into an upper shelf in the hall closet, the potato chips and snacks into the lower cabinets. We also put those latches on all of the cupboards and drawers, but Justin figured those out in about a week.

As he got older, Linda let him use the blender, the mixer, and other appliances—all with her supervision and all with hand-over-hand assistance. This meant that when he was two or three she would put his hand around the appliance or let him push the buttons on the microwave, mixer, or blender so he thought he was doing the task, but in reality, Linda had total control. Justin still got the feel of the appliance, and we made a fuss about what great food he had helped to prepare.

Justin also used a toy kitchen and a toy barbecue grill. We allowed him to use plastic serrated knives and plastic forks and spoons until we were comfortable with the fact that he knew the dangers of sharp objects. When he moved on to the real thing, it was again with hand-over-hand assistance until we knew he could control the utensils on his own. These are just a few hints we learned from our experience, but it's all common sense and observation. You'll be surprised how much fun it is for everyone when you let your child get involved. Remember, safety first. The parent takes control, kids love things that spin and pushing buttons, and if a mess is made, get them to help clean it up. Justin does dishes, too. Have fun.

Linda Miller   Jimi Miller

Linda and Jimi Miller
Chef Justin's Mom and Dad

Blast-Off Breakfasts

Hannah's Banana French Toast

2 eggs
$1/2$ cup milk
$3/4$ teaspoon cinnamon
1 banana cut into chunks
6 slices bread

Put all ingredients in blender, mix well.
Dip bread slices into batter for a few seconds.
Turn over.
Brown on both sides on heated nonstick griddle.

LEVEL OF DIFFICULTY

The blender is one of my favorite kitchen appliances.

Austin's Awesome French Toast

2 eggs
⅓ cup milk
⅛ teaspoon salt
4 slices bread, about 1 inch thick
cinnamon, syrup

Beat eggs with milk and salt in a shallow bowl.

Trim crusts from bread (optional).

Cut in half.

Dip in egg mixture for a few seconds and turn over.

Place on heated nonstick skillet.

Brown for about 2 minutes on each side.

Serve with maple syrup and sprinkle with cinnamon.

This is one of my favorites!

LEVEL OF DIFFICULTY

Cynthia's Cinnamon Swirls

1 package refrigerated pie crusts
1 tablespoon melted butter
2 tablespoons cinnamon (to taste)
1 box plain toothpicks

Place pie crusts flat on cookie sheet.

Brush with melted butter, both sides.

Sprinkle with cinnamon, both sides.

Roll up and cut into 1½-inch pieces.

Keep rolled-up pieces together with toothpicks.

Bake at 325 degrees for 8 to 9 minutes or until golden brown.

Serve and enjoy!

LEVEL OF DIFFICULTY

Brian's Fun Bubble Buns

¹/₃ **cup sugar**

³/₄ **teaspoon cinnamon**

³/₄ **cup finely chopped walnuts or pecans**

1 package refrigerated biscuits (10)

¹/₄ **cup mayonnaise**

Combine sugar, cinnamon, and nuts in a small bowl.

Separate biscuits, cut into quarters, and shape into balls.

Spread on mayonnaise.

Roll into nut mixture.

Place 4 balls in 10 greased muffin cups.

Bake at 400 degrees for 10 to 18 minutes or until browned.

LEVEL OF DIFFICULTY

Whitney's Wild Walnut Pancakes

2¼ cups biscuit mix
2 eggs
1 cup milk
¾ cup chopped walnuts

Beat eggs, milk, and biscuit mix in a large bowl.
Then add walnuts.
Pour ¼ cupful of batter onto nonstick griddle.
Cook until edges are dry.
Turn over.
Cook until golden brown.
Serve with maple syrup.

Makes about 13 pancakes.

LEVEL OF DIFFICULTY

Pappap Joe's Potato Pancakes

6 medium potatoes, cut into chunks

1 egg

2 tablespoons flour

1 small onion

Mix all ingredients in blender.

Pour 1/4 cupful of batter onto hot nonstick griddle.

Cook until edges are dry.

Turn over.

Cook until golden brown.

LEVEL OF DIFFICULTY

Amazing Grains!

Bridget's Biscuit Drops

2 cups flour
3$\frac{1}{8}$ teaspoons baking powder
$\frac{3}{4}$ teaspoon salt
$\frac{1}{4}$ cup shortening
1 cup milk

Mix all ingredients in a large bowl.
Drop by tablespoonfuls onto greased baking sheet.
Bake at 450 degrees for 11 to 13 minutes.

LEVEL OF DIFFICULTY

Nora's Nutty Knead
(Nut Bread)

4 cups flour

1 cup sugar

2 cups milk

1 cup chopped walnuts

4 teaspoons baking soda

2 eggs

1 teaspoon salt

Mix all ingredients in a large bowl.

Spread in 2 loaf pans, allow to rise 20 minutes.

Bake at 375 degrees for 45 minutes.

LEVEL OF DIFFICULTY

Jeffrey's Cheddary Cheese Bread

3¹/₃ cups biscuit mix
2³/₄ cups grated cheese
2 eggs beaten slightly
1¹/₄ cups milk

Combine biscuit mix and cheese in a large bowl.
In another bowl, mix together eggs and milk.
Stir into cheese mixture, just enough to moisten.
Grease and flour 9- x 5-inch loaf pan.
Bake at 350 degrees for 55 to 60 minutes.

LEVEL OF DIFFICULTY

Beth's Best Banana Bread

¹/₂ cup butter

1 cup sugar

2 cups flour

¹/₂ teaspoon salt

¹/₂ cup chopped walnuts or pecans

¹/₂ teaspoon baking powder

3 crushed bananas

2 eggs

Combine butter and sugar in a large bowl.

Blend flour, salt, walnuts, and baking powder.

Stir in bananas and eggs. Mix well.

Bake at 350 degrees for about 1 hour.

KNOCK, KNOCK!

Who's there?

Justin.

Justin who?

Justin case you're wondering, it's time to go.

LEVEL OF DIFFICULTY

Super Soups and Salads

Fran's Fruit Fiesta

1 3-ounce package orange Jell-O

1 8-ounce tub Cool Whip

1 15-ounce can mandarin oranges (drained)

1 12-ounce container small curd cottage cheese

1 small can pineapple chunks

Save a few pineapple chunks and a few oranges for garnish.

Make Jell-O according to package directions.

In a separate bowl, mix all other ingredients.

Stir Jell-O mix in with other ingredients.

Chill until ready to serve.

Garnish with reserved fruit.

Makes 6 to 8 servings.

LEVEL OF DIFFICULTY

Mitch's Spinach Salad

1½ pounds spinach leaves, washed and torn into pieces (no stems)

2 cups mushrooms, sliced

¼ cup fat-free Ranch or Italian dressing

Combine spinach, mushrooms, and tomatoes in salad bowl.

Pour on dressing, toss, and serve.

KNOCK, KNOCK!

Who's there?

Wooden shoe.

Wooden shoe who?

Wooden shoe like to know.

LEVEL OF DIFFICULTY

Marty's Hearty Spudsy Soup

4 cups diced potatoes

1 cup diced celery

1 medium onion, sliced

2 tablespoons fresh parsley

1 can mushrooms (drained)

4 vegetable or beef bouillon cubes

1/4 cup butter

1 cup sour cream

Cook potatoes, celery, onion, parsley, and mushrooms in 2 cups water in a large saucepan until done.

Separately add bouillon cubes to 2 cups hot water.

Add butter.

Pour over vegetables, and stir well.

Remove from heat.

Blend in sour cream.

Makes 4 to 6 servings.

KNOCK, KNOCK!

Who's there?
Soup.
Soup who?
Soup-erman.

LEVEL OF DIFFICULTY

Ernesto's Pesto Salad

8 ounces small pasta shells
2 cups fresh basil leaves (no stems)
1 cup fresh parsley
1 1/2 tablespoons pine nuts
3 cloves garlic, peeled
1 teaspoon salt
1/3 cup virgin olive oil
1/2 cup freshly grated Parmesan cheese

Cook pasta in boiling, salted water until tender. Drain.

Place basil, parsley, pine nuts, garlic, salt, and oil in food processor or blender and mix until smooth.

Place mixture in bowl and blend in Parmesan cheese.

Place in refrigerator until ready to serve.

Toss basil mixture with pasta and serve.

Makes 4 servings.

LEVEL OF DIFFICULTY

Grand Sandwiches

Jay Dog

8 hot dogs
8 strips cheddar cheese
1 package crescent rolls

Slit hot dogs lengthwise.
Put in cheese.
Place hot dog on small end of crescent roll and roll up.

Bake at 350 degrees for 12 minutes.

LEVEL OF DIFFICULTY

Emma's Easy Holiday Eats
(Turkey Sandwiches)

1 10½-ounce jar turkey gravy
4 large slices cooked turkey
4 hard rolls, sliced

In a large skillet, heat gravy to boil over medium heat.
Add turkey, reduce heat to low, until heated through.
Serve on rolls.
Makes 4 servings.

KNOCK, KNOCK!

Who's there?
Norma Lee.
Norma Lee who?
Norma Lee I'd be in bed by now.

LEVEL OF DIFFICULTY

Kurt's Turtle Sandwiches

6 baguette rolls, sliced
fresh spinach leaves
lettuce
1 medium cucumber, cut into rounds
1 medium green bell pepper, cut into strips
1 jar green or black olives (optional)

Cut roll in half, spoon out dough from rolls.

Lay in about 3 or 4 spinach leaves.

Top with lettuce, green pepper strips, cucumber rounds, and olives (I prefer the black).

Eat and enjoy.

Makes 12 servings.

LEVEL OF DIFFICULTY

(Note: I made this on Mister Rogers' Neighborhood)

Scott Dogs in a Blanket

1 16-ounce loaf frozen bread dough, thawed
1-pound package (10) hot dogs
ketchup and mustard

Divide dough into 10 portions.

On lightly floured surface, roll each portion into 10- x 2-inch rectangle.

Place hot dog lengthwise on each rectangle, about $3/4$ inch from end.

Spread hot dog with ketchup and mustard.

Fold dough over to cover three-quarters of each hot dog.

Moisten edges with water.

Press together to seal.

Place on greased baking sheet.

Cover and let dough rise in a warm place for 30 minutes.

Bake at 375 degrees for 16 to 18 minutes till golden brown.

LEVEL OF DIFFICULTY

Sydney's Sailing Ships

4 small hard rolls
1 cup diced, cooked ham
1/4 cup chopped celery
3 tablespoons mayonnaise
1 1/2 tablespoons chopped onion
dash black pepper
1 slice American cheese, cut into 4 squares

Cut rolls in half.
Scoop out dough, leaving 1/4-inch shell.
In medium bowl, combine ham, celery, onion, and pepper.
Spoon meat mixture into center of rolls.

To make sails, thread 1 piece of cheese on a toothpick.
Stick into roll.

LEVEL OF DIFFICULTY

Poke Annie's Salad

2 large pita bread, cut in half

1 cup shredded lettuce

1 medium cucumber, sliced into half moons

1 small carrot, sliced into rounds

6 radishes, sliced into rounds

1 medium green bell pepper, sliced into strips

1 medium tomato, sliced into rounds, then quartered

1 cup sweet or sour pickles, sliced

5 pieces American cheese

2 tablespoons Ranch dressing

Mix all ingredients, except dressing, in a medium bowl.

Toss together.

Stuff each pocket with filling.

Spoon on dressing.

Eat immediately.

Makes 4 servings.

LEVEL OF DIFFICULTY

Pick-Me-Up Snacks and Sides

Aunt Lori's Marvelous Muffins

4 English muffins, sliced in half

8 tablespoons tomato sauce

4 tablespoons dry oregano

8 tablespoons grated mozzarella cheese

Spread 1 tablespoon tomato sauce on each muffin.

Sprinkle oregano and 1 tablespoon cheese on each muffin.

Place in baking dish.

Bake at 350 degrees for 10 minutes.

LEVEL OF DIFFICULTY

Mark's
Shark Attack
(Eggs)

6 hard-boiled eggs

1 6½-ounce can tuna (drained)

1 small onion, chopped

2 tablespoons mayonnaise

1 shake salt

1 shake pepper

2 shakes paprika

Slice eggs in half.

Scoop out yolks into a medium mixing bowl.

Add tuna and break with fork.

Stir in onions, mayonnaise, salt, and pepper until blended.

Fill egg whites with mixture.

Shake on paprika.

KNOCK, KNOCK!

Who's there?

Anaconda.

Anaconda who?

Anaconda you, I'm still on the porch.

LEVEL OF DIFFICULTY

51

Robin's Hoppin' Popovers

1 cup milk
1 cup flour
2 eggs
$1/4$ teaspoon salt

Mix all ingredients in a medium bowl until blended.
Batter will be lumpy.
Pour into well-greased custard cups.
Fill only half full
Place in cold oven.
Set oven to 450 degrees, and bake for 30 minutes.

LEVEL OF DIFFICULTY

Tom's Ever-so-Nice Rice
(Cheese and Tomato Rice)

1 16-ounce can of stewed tomatoes
1½ tablespoons butter
½ cup water
1⅓ cups minute rice
½ cup Parmesan cheese, freshly grated

Combine tomatoes, butter, and water in a medium saucepan.

Bring to a boil.

Stir in rice, cover.

Remove from heat.

Let stand for 5 minutes.

Stir in cheese.

Serve hot.

LEVEL OF DIFFICULTY

Miranda's Tie-Dyed Marbles

4 hard-boiled eggs

1 envelope each, grape, cherry, orange, lemon-lime drink mix

Tap eggs until shells are cracked all around, do not remove shells.

In small bowls, dissolve drink mixes in 3 cups cold water.

Add cracked eggs.

Put in refrigerator overnight.

Remove eggs and throw away liquid.

Peel eggs and store in refrigerator until ready to serve.

LEVEL OF DIFFICULTY

Stephanie's Stellar Stuffed Celery

1 stalk celery
1 package cream cheese
salt, pepper, and paprika

Wash and cut celery into bite-size pieces (about 3 inches).

Spread cream cheese into groove of celery with butter knife.

Add salt and pepper to taste.

Sprinkle with paprika.

Go Veggies!

KNOCK, KNOCK!

Who's there?

Euripedes.

Euripedes who?

Euripedes pants and you're in trouble.

LEVEL OF DIFFICULTY

Mrs. Zigerell's Zucchini Rings

2 small or medium zucchini

1 teaspoon butter

2 tablespoons water

1 shake salt

1 shake pepper

2 teaspoons grated Parmesan cheese

Cut zucchini into 1/4-inch rounds.

Heat a large skillet to medium hot.

Melt butter.

Add water.

Place zucchini in skillet.

Stir until tender and crisp (this takes about 5 minutes).

Season with salt and pepper.

Melt cheese on top of zucchini while cooking.

This is a yummy veggie!

LEVEL OF DIFFICULTY

Chris P. Crunch

1 package frozen green beans, thawed
½ cup seasoned bread crumbs
¼ cup butter
½ small onion, chopped

In a large skillet, melt butter.

Add green beans.

Mix until beans are coated with butter.

Put bread crumbs over top.

Cook on medium-high heat until crumbs are toasted and crisp.

Add onions until just tender and crisp.

Serve hot.

LEVEL OF DIFFICULTY

Courtney's Crunchy Crumblies
(Zucchini and Cheese)

$1/2$ cup cornflake crumbs

$2 1/2$ tablespoons freshly grated Parmesan cheese

$1/4$ teaspoon seasoned salt

1 pinch garlic powder

5 small, unpeeled zucchini, cut into 3-inch strips

$1/4$ cup melted butter

Combine crumbs, cheese, and seasonings in a small bowl.

Dip zucchini in butter and coat with crumb mixture.

Bake at 375 degrees for 10 minutes or until crisp.

LEVEL OF DIFFICULTY

Max's Mad Spuds

4 pounds potatoes peeled, cut into cubes
2³/₄ tablespoons salted butter
3¹/₂ onions, chopped
1¹/₂ tablespoons paprika
¹/₂ teaspoon salt

Steam potatoes in a large covered saucepan and steamer basket 14 to 18 minutes until tender.

Melt butter in skillet over medium heat.

Add onions.

Heat 8 to 10 minutes until tender.

Remove from heat.

Combine all ingredients except paprika.

Mash thoroughly.

Sprinkle with paprika and serve.

KNOCK, KNOCK!
(make circle with right hand in the air)
Who's there?
Ya.
Ya-who?

LEVEL OF DIFFICULTY

Fabulous Fruits

Adam's Apple Smileys

1 red apple, cored and sliced
peanut butter
miniature marshmallows

Spread peanut butter on one side of apple slice.
Place 4 marshmallows on the peanut butter.
Top with another apple slice.
Squeeze together gently.

Makes 8 to 10.

LEVEL OF DIFFICULTY

Aunt Rita's Pushcoal

3 eggs

1 cup sugar

1 tablespoon fresh lemon juice

4 tablespoons canned strawberries

1 tablespoon strawberry extract

1 cup marshmallows

1 12-ounce container whipped topping

In a medium saucepan, mix eggs, sugar, lemon juice, strawberry extract, and strawberries over medium heat.

Stir in marshmallows until melted.

Cool completely.

Blend in whipped topping.

Stir until smooth.

Dip cantaloupe, honeydew melons, cherries, strawberries, pineapple, and apples.

Dip fruit in stuff and have fun!

LEVEL OF DIFFICULTY

Jimmy Roach's Apple Dip

6½ ounces cream cheese, softened
30 graham crackers (in 2½-inch squares)
1 can apple pie filling

Spread about 1¼ teaspoons cream cheese on each cracker.

Place 1 tablespoon pie filling in centers of 15 crackers.

Save 15 apple slices.

Top with remaining crackers and apple slices.

LEVEL OF DIFFICULTY

Johnny's Legendary Applesauce

7–8 cooking apples, peeled, cored, and quartered
1/2 cup water
1/2 cup brown sugar
1/2 teaspoon cinnamon

Place apples and water in a 2-quart glass casserole dish.

Cover with tight-fitting lid or plastic wrap.

Microwave on high for 8 to 10 minutes or until apples are soft.

Stir halfway through cooking.

Place apple mixture in blender or food processor.

Add sugar and cinnamon while still hot.

Blend until smooth.

LEVEL OF DIFFICULTY

Delicious Main Dishes

Kirk's Perky Turkey Toes

8 long pieces turkey

3 tablespoons milk

3 ounces cream cheese

1 medium onion, chopped

8 ounces sour cream

1 can cream of chicken soup

1 package crescent rolls

Heat milk and cream cheese in a large skillet.

Add turkey until thoroughly heated.

Add onion.

Cook until turkey is tender.

Prepare crescent rolls according to package instructions.

Cut rolls in half lengthwise and place mixture inside.

For sauce: Heat soup and sour cream in a small saucepan until smooth.

When rolls are finished baking, spoon sauce over top.

LEVEL OF DIFFICULTY

Rob's Gobba Gob Gobbler
(Thanksgiving Leftover Casserole)

2 pounds turkey (white or dark meat), cut into pieces

1 can cream of chicken soup

3 cups leftover stuffing

1 package frozen or leftover mashed potatoes

2¹/₃ cups milk

In a large skillet, brown pieces of turkey.

Add cream of chicken soup and 1 can water to turkey. Simmer.

Prepare mashed potatoes in a 4-inch-high baking dish according to package directions.

When potatoes are done, top them with stuffing, then pour turkey mixture over top of stuffing.

Preheat oven to 350 degrees and bake for 25 minutes.

Makes 4 to 5 servings.

LEVEL OF DIFFICULTY

Pappap Wally's Pork Chops

5 large pork chops
1 medium onion, chopped
1 can cream of mushroom soup
1 10-ounce package frozen green beans

Cook pork chops in a large skillet until very brown.
Place chops in shallow baking dish with all ingredients.
Bake covered at 350 degrees for 1½ to 2 hours.

LEVEL OF DIFFICULTY

Bradner's Broc-n-Role
(Broccoli Casserole)

1 stick butter or margarine

1 onion, chopped

1 package frozen broccoli spears

1 can cream of chicken or mushroom soup

1/2 can milk (use empty soup can)

1 pound cheddar cheese, cubed

1 cup cooked rice

KNOCK, KNOCK!

Who's there?

Cargo.

Cargo who?

Car go beep beep.

In a large heated skillet, melt butter and cook onion and broccoli spears.

Add soup, milk, and cheese.

When cheese is melted, add rice.

Transfer to a casserole dish, cover, and bake at 350 degrees for 15 minutes.

LEVEL OF DIFFICULTY

Renee's Sautéed Saupé
(Sausage, Potatoes, and Peppers)

1 tablespoon oil
1 pound sweet or hot sausage
2 large green and red bell peppers, cut into ½-inch strips
1 pound potatoes, peeled and diced (about 3 cups)
1 envelope dried onion soup mix
1½ cups water

In a large skillet, heat oil over medium-high heat and brown sausage. Remove sausage, cut into 1-inch chunks, and set aside. Reserve drippings.

Add peppers to drippings and cook over high heat.

Reduce heat, cover, and let simmer 10 minutes.

Return sausage to skillet and simmer covered for 5 minutes, or until sausage is done and potatoes are tender.

Serve with hot, crusty Italian bread.

Serves 4.

LEVEL OF DIFFICULTY

Luke's Put Up Your Zukes
(Zucchini Sauce and Pasta)

Explore the Pastabilities!

1 medium onion, chopped

1 small or medium zucchini, sliced

1 14½-ounce can chopped seasoned tomatoes (half drained)

1 tablespoon bottled pesto sauce

½ pound spaghetti

2 tablespoons freshly grated Parmesan cheese

Combine onion, zucchini, and tomatoes in a large nonstick saucepan.

Cover and simmer 15 minutes.

Remove cover and simmer 10 minutes, until sauce begins to thicken.

Stir in pesto and set aside.

While sauce is cooking, cook pasta according to package directions.

Drain pasta.

Toss with zucchini sauce and Parmesan cheese in a large bowl.

LEVEL OF DIFFICULTY

Uncle Dale's Springs

1 box spring macaroni
1 pound ground round
1 medium onion, chopped
1 large can tomato juice
1/2 cup freshly grated Parmesan cheese

While macaroni is cooking, brown ground beef in a large skillet and drain well.

Add onion and cook until tender.

Cook macaroni according to package directions.

Add tomato juice and cheese to meat mixture.

Add cooked macaroni.

Simmer 20 minutes.

LEVEL OF DIFFICULTY

Scu B. Doodles
(Italian Noodles)

1 half-pound bag egg noodles
$1/2$ cup melted butter
$1/2$ tablespoon heavy cream
$1^1/_4$ cups freshly grated Parmesan cheese
$1/4$ teaspoon garlic powder
1 small onion, chopped
oregano

In large pot, boil salted water.

Add noodles, and cook until just tender.

While noodles are cooking, melt butter in a small saucepan, add cream and cheese.

Stir until smooth, do not boil.

Drain noodles well, pour into large bowl.

Pour sauce over noodles.

Toss with fork and mix well.

Sprinkle with oregano (optional).

LEVEL OF DIFFICULTY

Marvin's Garden Chicken

1 pound boneless, skinless chicken breasts, cubed

1 medium onion chopped

1 1-pound bag frozen broccoli, carrots, and cauliflower

1 10³/₄-ounce can condensed cream of chicken soup

2 tablespoons water

¹/₂ cup sour cream

2-3 cups hot cooked noodles

Coat a large skillet with nonstick cooking spray.

Cook chicken and onion over medium-high heat until chicken is brown, stirring occasionally.

Add vegetables, soup, and water. Mix well.

Reduce heat to low, cover, and simmer 10 minutes until vegetables are tender and crisp, stirring occasionally. Remove from heat.

Stir in sour cream and noodles.

Salt and pepper to taste.

Makes 4 to 5 servings.

LEVEL OF DIFFICULTY

Mr. Blue's Groovin' Tuna

1 6½-ounce can tuna fish, drained
2 tablespoons chopped onion
1 tablespoon chopped celery
¼ teaspoon black pepper
1 box Ritz crackers

In a medium bowl, mix tuna, onion, celery, and pepper.

Spread on crackers.

Something's Fishy Here . . .

KNOCK, KNOCK!

Who's there?
Wire.
Wire who?
Wire you looking at me like that?

LEVEL OF DIFFICULTY

Danny's Tune-a-Fish
(Tuna Rice)

1 chicken bouillon cube
1³/₄ cups hot water
1 frozen package sweet peas
1 10-ounce can condensed cheddar cheese soup
2 cans tuna fish, drained
1¹/₃ cups minute rice

Dissolve bouillon cube in hot water in a large saucepan.

Add peas, bring to a boil.

Add soup, stir until smooth.

Add tuna and rice, bring back to a boil.

Cover, remove from heat.

Let stand for 5 minutes.

Serve.

Makes 4 servings.

LEVEL OF DIFFICULTY

Fishbowl Allie

1 pound fish fillets cod, perch, sole (fresh or frozen)
1 cup canned tomatoes
2 tablespoons chopped onion
$1/2$ teaspoon salt
1 tablespoon black pepper
2 tablespoons chopped fresh parsley
$1^1/_2$ tablespoons grated Parmesan cheese

Preheat oven to 400 degrees.

Wash and dry fish.

Place tomatoes in bottom of shallow baking dish.

Place fish over tomatoes in single layer.

Sprinkle with onion and half of salt.

Top with parsley, pepper, remaining salt, and finally with Parmesan cheese.

Cover with foil and bake for 20 minutes.

Makes 4 servings.

LEVEL OF DIFFICULTY

Barnyard Best

Charlie's Cheddared Chicken

2 pounds skinless, boneless chicken breasts

2 tablespoons butter

1 11-ounce can condensed cheddar cheese soup

³/₄ cups canned chopped tomatoes

¹/₄ teaspoon chopped fresh basil leaves

In a large skillet, slowly brown chicken in butter for about 30 minutes.

Add remaining ingredients.

Cover, cook over low heat for 15 minutes or until tender, stirring occasionally.

LEVEL OF DIFFICULTY

Kelly's Cluckers
(Creamy Chicken and Vegetables)

4 skinless, boneless chicken breasts
1/4 teaspoon garlic powder
1 10³/4 ounce can cream of mushroom soup
1/2 cup milk
1/2 teaspoon dried or fresh basil leaves, crushed
1 16-ounce bag frozen mixed vegetables

Sprinkle chicken with garlic powder.

Coat a large skillet with cooking spray.

Heat over medium-high heat 1 minute.

Cook chicken 10 minutes or until browned.

Set chicken aside.

Add soup, milk, basil, and vegetables to skillet.

Heat to boil.

Return chicken to skillet.

Cover and cook over low heat for 10 minutes or until chicken is done.

Makes 4 servings.

> **KNOCK, KNOCK!**
> Who's there?
> *Phil.*
> Phil who?
> *Phil 'er up before the tank goes empty.*

LEVEL OF DIFFICULTY

Phil's Cool-as-a-Cucumber Canoe

1 cucumber, peeled
1 cooked chicken breast, chopped
¼ cup mayonnaise
1 small onion, chopped
1 stalk celery, chopped
4 cherry tomatoes with toothpicks

In a small skillet, cook chicken breast until tender.

In a small bowl, mix onion, celery, and mayonnaise.

Add mixture to chicken breast.

Cut cucumber in half lengthwise and scoop out seeds.

Place mixture inside cucumber.

Place cherry tomatoes on top of cucumber.

Insert toothpick on top of each tomato.

Insert a toothpick on both sides of the tomatoes to make them look like oars.

Crunchy and healthy!

LEVEL OF DIFFICULTY

Lucy's Lunar Logs
(Chicken Crescent Roll-Ups)

1 pound chicken breasts, cut into chunks

1 package crescent rolls

1 medium onion, chopped

3 ounces cream cheese

3 tablespoons milk

Brown chicken in a large skillet.

Add onion, cream cheese, and milk.

Heat until onion is tender and cream cheese is melted.

Open crescent rolls and pull apart.

Place 2 pieces of chicken and onion mixture onto each roll.

Roll up and close ends.

Bake at 350 degrees for 20 minutes.

For Sauce:

1 can cream of chicken soup

8 ounces sour cream

Heat in medium saucepan until smooth.

Spoon over finished chicken roll-up.

LEVEL OF DIFFICULTY

81

Joey's Pouch Pals

1 package crescent rolls
3/4 pound thin-sliced corned beef
1/2 pound Swiss cheese
1 can sauerkraut
1/4 cup Thousand Islands dressing

Make rectangles with two sections of crescent rolls.

Layer corned beef, cheese, and sauerkraut on rectangles.

Add dressing.

Roll up and pinch ends closed.

Bake at 325 degrees for 15 minutes, until bread is golden brown and cheese is melted and bubbly.

LEVEL OF DIFFICULTY

Taylor's Tasty Tater Tots

¹/₂-1 cup chopped onion
1 pound ground beef
1 10¹/₂-ounce can cream of celery soup
4 cups frozen Tater Tots

Preheat oven to 400 degrees.

Grease shallow 2-quart baking dish.

In 10-inch skillet over medium-high heat, cook onions and ground beef until meat is well done.

Drain fat.

Spread meat mixture in baking dish, cover with undiluted soup, and top with single layer of frozen Tater Tots.

Bake for 45 minutes, until hot and bubbly in center.

Makes 4 to 5 servings.

LEVEL OF DIFFICULTY

Paco's Taco

1 pound ground beef

1 envelope taco seasoning

1 can refried beans

16 ounces sour cream

1 8-ounce bottle salsa (hot, medium, or mild)

2 packages grated cheddar cheese

In a large skillet, brown meat, drain well.

Combine meat, seasoning, and beans.

Place meat mixture into pie pan and press with spoon to shape like crust.

Mix sour cream and salsa together in a medium bowl and cover meat mixture.

Top with cheese, cover with foil, and bake at 350 degrees for 30 minutes.

Serve with nacho chips.

LEVEL OF DIFFICULTY

Karen's Karousel

1 pound lean ground beef
1 small can chopped tomatoes
³/₄ cup water
1 package frozen seasoned Italian vegetables
1¹/₄ cups cooked rice

Brown beef in a large skillet, drain well.

Add tomatoes, water, and vegetables.

Bring to a boil.

Separate vegetables with fork, stirring until blended.

Cover and simmer 3 minutes, and boil.

Stir in rice.

Cover and remove from heat.

Let stand 5 minutes.

Serve immediately.

LEVEL OF DIFFICULTY

Your
Just(in's)
Desserts

Natalie's Nut and Honey Butterballs

³/₄ cup sugar

1 cup honey

1¹/₄ cups chunk-style peanut butter

5 cups popped popcorn

In a medium saucepan, boil sugar and honey for 1¹/₂ minutes.

Stir in peanut butter until melted, pour over popped corn.

Rub butter on your hands and piece mixture into balls.

Makes about 1 dozen.

LEVEL OF DIFFICULTY

Mallory's Mellow Mix
(Fudgemallow Candy)

1 12-ounce package semisweet chocolate morsels
1 cup chunk-style peanut butter
4 cups miniature marshmallows

Melt chocolate morsels with peanut butter in medium saucepan over low heat, stirring until smooth.

Fold in marshmallows.

Pour into a greased 9-inch-square pan.

Chill until firm, cut into squares.

Makes about 2 dozen.

KNOCK, KNOCK!

Who's there?
Tuba.
Tuba who?
Tuba toothpaste.

LEVEL OF DIFFICULTY

Liz's Frosty Fizz
(Chocolate Bubbles)

2¼ cups milk
¾ cup chocolate syrup
1 pint vanilla ice cream
2½ cups chilled sparkling water

In a medium bowl, combine milk and syrup, mix well.

Divide mixture into four 12-ounce glasses.

Top each glass with 1 scoop ice cream.

Fill each glass with sparkling water and stir.

Serve immediately.

Optional: When done, top with chocolate whipped topping and sprinkles.

Makes 4 servings.

LEVEL OF DIFFICULTY

Jane's Rainbow Teasers

1 bag microwave popcorn, popped

$1/2$ cup candy-coated chocolate (M&M's)

$1/2$ cup peanuts

$2^1/_3$ cups miniature marshmallows

$1/_4$ cup margarine

$1/_4$ cup raisins (optional)

In greased bowl, combine popcorn, M&M's, peanuts, and raisins (optional).

Melt marshmallows and margarine in a medium saucepan.

Pour mixture over popcorn mix.

Toss until well coated.

Rub batter on your hands and press mixture into balls.

For gift-giving, wrap individually in colored or clear plastic

Try this one out during the holidays!

LEVEL OF DIFFICULTY

Patty's Peppermint Brownies

1 box brownie mix

³/₄ cup chopped walnuts

20 small peppermint patties

Make cake-like brownies according to package directions, using walnuts.

Turn off oven when done.

Place peppermint patties on top, soften in warm oven with door closed about 3 minutes, just enough to spread.

Cut when cool.

LEVEL OF DIFFICULTY

Caroline's Caramel Cozies

1 package vanilla or chocolate caramels
1/2 cup milk
4 cups rice cereal
1 1/4 cups salted peanuts
16 icicle-type wooden sticks

In a 3-quart saucepan, combine caramels and milk.

Stir over low heat until melted and smooth.

Remove from heat.

Stir in cereal and peanuts until well coated.

In greased square baking pan, spoon in mixture.

Let stand for 1 hour until firm.

Cut firm mixture into 2-inch squares.

Insert wooden stick into one end of square.

Makes 16.

LEVEL OF DIFFICULTY

Dougie's Delicious Dough

4 cups flour

1 cup water

2$1/4$ teaspoons baking powder

1 dash salt

oil

cinnamon or powdered sugar (optional)

In a large bowl, mix flour, water, baking powder, and salt until well blended.

Knead 1 or 2 minutes.

Cover in a large bowl and let rise 25 minutes.

Pat bread out to $1/2$-inch thick.

Cut into triangles.

Cut 1-inch slit in middle of each.

Heat 1$1/3$ inches of oil in large electric skillet.

Fry until golden brown.

Sprinkle with powdered sugar and cinnamon, or with one or the other.

Eat and enjoy!

LEVEL OF DIFFICULTY

Emily's Lemmaries

1 can lemon pie filling
1¼ cups sour cream
6 shortcake shells
1 pint fresh berries (strawberries or blueberries)

In a medium bowl, combine pie filling and sour cream.
Divide among shells evenly.
Top each with fresh berries.

Makes 6 servings.

LEVEL OF DIFFICULTY

The Bozada Brothers' Banana Blast

1 large banana
1¹/₂ cups milk
1¹/₂ cups chocolate ice cream
¹/₂ cup creamy peanut butter

Cut banana into 1-inch rounds.

Wrap in foil and freeze.

When frozen, unwrap and combine with milk, ice cream, and peanut butter in blender.

Blend until smooth.

Makes three 6-ounce servings.

LEVEL OF DIFFICULTY

Flo's Fruity Floats

2¹/₂ cups milk

¹/₂ pint peach ice cream

1 package frozen peaches, thawed (reserve some slices for top)

¹/₄ teaspoon vanilla extract

1 small tub whipped topping

Combine first 4 ingredients in blender.

Mix until smooth.

Pour into glasses.

Top with whipped topping, and 1 or 2 peach slices.

KNOCK, KNOCK!

Who's there?

Orange.

Orange who?

Orange you glad I came to see you?

LEVEL OF DIFFICULTY

97

Very Cherry Gamble

24 chocolate wafer cookies

2¹/₂ cups sour cream

1 can cherry pie filling

8 dessert dishes

In each dish, layer 1 chocolate wafer.

Add generous tablespoon of sour cream.

Add one tablespoon pie filling.

Repeat with 2 additional layers.

Chill about 60 to 70 minutes before serving.

LEVEL OF DIFFICULTY

Rudy's Fruity Fog

⅔ cup mayonnaise
1 cup sour cream
1 can cherry pie filling

In a small bowl, fold in mayonnaise and sour cream.

Add pie filling.

Spoon into 6 mold cups and freeze.

Before serving, remove from mold.

Place on dish.

Garnish with parsley.

Optional:

Place fresh cherries in between parsley around dish.

LEVEL OF DIFFICULTY

Isaac's Chapple Freeze

1 can cherry pie filling
1 can sweetened condensed milk
1 small can pineapple chunks
1 8-ounce tub whipped topping

In a large bowl, combine pie filling, milk, and pineapple.
Blend in half a tub of whipped topping.
Spoon mixture in muffin tin lined with paper cups.
Freeze about 2$\frac{1}{2}$ hours.
Before serving, top with remaining whipped topping.

Do not use evaporated milk!

LEVEL OF DIFFICULTY

Yogi-Berries

1¹/₂ quarts vanilla yogurt
1¹/₂ cups hot fudge topping
6 cups fresh strawberries, washed and halved

Combine yogurt and fudge topping in a large bowl, mix well.

Place berries in individual serving bowls.

Top with chocolate cream.

Option: Place 1¹/₂ tablespoons whipped topping in bottom of serving bowls.

KNOCK, KNOCK!

Who's there?

The impatient cow.

The impatient cow who?

(Say, "moo" before they finish.)

LEVEL OF DIFFICULTY

101

Harry's Banana Hunks

1¹/₂ tablespoons peanut butter
¹/₂ cup butterscotch morsels
2 medium bananas, peeled
¹/₂ cup finely chopped peanuts

In a small saucepan, combine peanut butter and butterscotch morsels.

Cook over low heat, stirring constantly until melted and smooth.

Cut bananas into 1–1¹/₂ inch rounds.

Dip each piece of banana into butterscotch mixture.

Remove with fork.

Roll banana pieces in chopped peanuts until covered.

Place on wax paper and plate.

Chill 2 hours.

Makes 2 to 3 servings.

LEVEL OF DIFFICULTY

Billy's Smashing Pumpkin Bars

4 large eggs

1³/₄ cups sugar

1 cup cooking oil

2 cups solid-pack pumpkin

2 cups all-purpose flour

2 teaspoons baking powder

1 teaspoon salt

2 teaspoons pumpkin pie spice

1 cup golden raisins

walnuts

Preheat oven to 350 degrees.

In mixer, beat eggs until frothy.

Beat in sugar for 2 minutes.

Beat in oil and pumpkin.

In a medium bowl, sift dry ingredients over raisins.

Fold dry mixture into egg mixture. Do not overmix.

Pour into greased and floured 13- by 9-inch pan .

Bake for 35 to 40 minutes.

Cool on rack and cut into 24 squares.

Top each square with toasted walnut.

LEVEL OF DIFFICULTY

Monstrously Good Cookies

Aunt Donna's Alien Eaties

1 stick butter

¹/₂ cup of milk

3 tablespoons cocoa

1 teaspoon vanilla

3 cups quick-cooking oats

¹/₂ cup peanut butter

In a medium saucepan, melt butter.

Add sugar and cocoa and boil 4 to 5 minutes.

Take off burner and add peanut butter.

Add vanilla and oats.

Drop mixture by teaspoonful onto wax paper.

Cool in refrigerator 10 to 15 minutes.

LEVEL OF DIFFICULTY

Uncle Bill's Peanut Butter Cookies

1 egg
1 cup sugar
1 cup peanut butter

Blend ingredients with electric mixer.

Take teaspoon of mixture and roll into a ball.

Place on ungreased cookie sheet.

Press down on ball with floured fork to make an X on top.

Bake at 350 degrees for 8 to 10 minutes.

KNOCK, KNOCK!

Who's there?

Venom.

Venom who?

Venom knocking on your door you're supposed to let me in.

LEVEL OF DIFFICULTY

105

Tracy's Crazy Cookies
(Peanut Butter Cookies)

1 egg
1 cup sugar
1 cup peanut butter
1 tablespoon flour
chocolate kisses

Mix all ingredients in a large bowl.

Spoon out dough by teaspoons.

Roll dough into balls.

Place on cookie sheet.

Press dough balls with fork dipped in flour.

Bake at 325 degrees for 8 to 10 minutes.

Before cookies cool, press chocolate kiss into center.

LEVEL OF DIFFICULTY

Uncle Joe's Brokers Cookies
(Potato Chip Cookies)

1 cup sugar

2 sticks butter

2 teaspoons vanilla extract

3 1/2 cups flour

2 cups crushed potato chips

powdered sugar

In a large bowl, cream sugar and butter together.

Add vanilla and dry ingredients.

Drop mixture by teaspoonful onto ungreased
cookie sheet.

Bake at 350 degrees for 20 minutes.

Cool on paper towel.

Sprinkle with powdered sugar.

LEVEL OF DIFFICULTY

Plenty of Pudding

Nanni Betty's Super Flip

1 large box vanilla pudding
1 can peach pie filling

In a saucepan, make pudding according to package directions, then chill.
In five parfait glasses, alternate pudding and pie filling.
Save some peach slices for top.

Optional:
On very top layer, put a tablespoon of whipped topping around edge of glass, then place slice of peach in the middle.

LEVEL OF DIFFICULTY

The Other Justin's Fluffy Fog

1 box chocolate pudding

3 cups milk

1 8-ounce tub whipped topping

sprinkles (optional)

Beat pudding and milk with electric mixer until thick.

Place in parfait glass sideways, alternating pudding and whipped cream until filled.

Chill about 1 hour.

KNOCK, KNOCK!

Who's there?

Freeze.

Freeze who?

Freeze a jolly good fellow.

I like to put sprinkles on top.

LEVEL OF DIFFICULTY

Skyler's Brown Parachutes

1 box cake mix (any flavor)
1 box banana instant pudding
powdered sugar

Make cupcakes according to package directions.
When cool, cut small circle from top of cupcakes.
Fill with pudding until just overflowing.
Place circle back on top (don't press in).
Sprinkle with powdered sugar.

LEVEL OF DIFFICULTY

Nanni Tina's Mini Puffs

1 cup water
1 stick butter
1 cup flour
4 eggs
1 box vanilla pudding (prepare as per box)

Boil water in a medium saucepan.

Add butter and flour.

Let cool.

Add eggs one at a time. Mix well.

Drop onto ungreased pan by teaspoonful.

Bake at 350 degrees for 15 minutes.

When done, cool and put a small hole in each one.

Fill with cooked vanilla pudding.

LEVEL OF DIFFICULTY

Amanda's Panda Pudding
(Creamy Rice Pudding)

3/4 cup rice

3 cups water

1/2 teaspoon salt

1 15-ounce can
    condensed milk

1/2 cup butter (1 stick)

1 tablespoon vanilla
    extract

1 can pie filling (cherry,
    blueberry, or peach)

whipped cream

mint leaf

Measure rice, water, and salt into a medium saucepan.

Bring to a boil, reduce heat to simmer, cook uncovered for 20 minutes.

Place rice in top of a double broiler, stir in milk and butter. Cook in double broiler until mixture thickens, about 20 minutes. Remove from heat and stir in vanilla.

Spoon into parfait glasses in alternate layers of rice pudding and pie filling.

Top with whipped cream. Garnish with mint leaf.

Makes 6 servings.

LEVEL OF DIFFICULTY

Derek's Demon Drops

1 box cake mix (yellow or white)
1 can cherry pie filling
1 tub whipped topping

Bake cake according to package directions.

Let cool.

Top with pie filling.

Drop whipped topping by spoonfuls on each serving.

LEVEL OF DIFFICULTY

Di's Flutter-By Pie

1 cup powdered sugar

1 3-ounce package soft cream cheese

¹/₂ cup peanut butter

1 graham cracker pie shell

Mix ingredients in blender for 4 minutes on medium speed.

Spread mixture into pie shell.

Freeze for 4 hours.

LEVEL OF DIFFICULTY

Shea's Strawberry Cheesecake Munchies

¹/₂ cup fresh strawberries
1 tub soft cream cheese
1 box Vanilla Wafers

Place strawberries in blender, blend until chopped.

Remove and combine with cream cheese in a small bowl. Mix well.

Spread on Vanilla Wafer on flat side.

Top with another wafer.

Eat right away!

LEVEL OF DIFFICULTY

Sam's Patriotic Flag Cake

2 pints strawberries

**1 10³/₄-ounce frozen pound cake, thawed, cut into 10
slices**

1¹/₃ cups blueberries

1 12-ounce tub Cool Whip, thawed

Slice 1 cup of strawberries, set aside. Halve remaining
strawberries, also set aside.

Line bottom of 12- x 8-inch baking dish with cake slices.

Top with 1 cup sliced strawberries, 1 cup blueberries, and
all of the Cool Whip.

Place strawberry halves and remaining blueberries on
whipped topping to create a flag design.

Refrigerate until ready to serve.

Makes 15 servings.

LEVEL OF DIFFICULTY

Halley's Chocolate Comet

1 box chocolate cake mix
1 can white ready-to-spread frosting
1 box chocolate mint cookies

Bake cake according to package directions. Let cool.

Frost top and sides.

Place mint cookies around top and sides if desired.

Use leftover frosting to make smiley faces on cookies.

KNOCK, KNOCK!

Who's there?
Pizza.
Pizza who?
Pizza nice guy once you get to know him.

LEVEL OF DIFFICULTY

Great Lamapple Cake

1 box spice cake mix
3 eggs
1 can apple pie filling

In a large mixing bowl, combine all ingredients.

Spread in greased cake pan (9 x 13 inches).

Bake at 350 degrees for 40 minutes.

Frost top with vanilla icing or sprinkle with powdered sugar.

LEVEL OF DIFFICULTY

Carrie's Cherry Mountain

2 cups powdered sugar
2¹/₂ cups flour
1 cup margarine or butter
1¹/₂ teaspoon vanilla extract
3 eggs
1 can cherry pie filling

Mix all ingredients in a large bowl, except pie filling.

Beat on low speed of electric mixer.

Beat until fluffy.

Pour ³/₄ of batter into greased 9- x 13-cake pan.

Spread pie filling over top.

Drop teaspoons of remaining batter over top.

Bake at 375 degrees for 45 minutes.

LEVEL OF DIFFICULTY

Monty's Funky Monkey
(Cherry Ice Cream Pie)

1 quart ice cream, slightly soft
1 graham cracker crust
1 can cherry pie filling
1 small tub whipped topping

In a large mixing bowl, stir half of the ice cream and spread evenly into crust.

Top with half of the pie filling.

Freeze about 50 to 55 minutes or until partway frozen.

Stir rest of ice cream in bowl and spread over top.

Freeze about 2$\frac{1}{2}$ hours.

Right before serving, top with remaining pie filling.

Drop tablespoon of whipped topping on each serving.

Serves 6.

Optional: Use chocolate crust.

LEVEL OF DIFFICULTY

Yvonne's Volcanoes

12 flat-bottom ice-cream cones

1 layer-size golden yellow cake mix

1 cup ready-spread frosting

1/4 cup crushed peanuts or miniature semisweet
  chocolate morsels

6 8-inch plastic drinking straws

Place ice-cream cones in a muffin pan.

Prepare cake batter according to package directions.

Fill each cone to within 1 inch of top.

Bake at 350 degrees for 30 minutes.

Remove from pan, cool completely.

Cover top of cakes with frosting. Sprinkle with nuts or
chocolate morsels.

Cut each straw into 4 pieces.

Insert 2 pieces into top of each cake, to make it look like
a soda.

LEVEL OF DIFFICULTY

Deanna's Banana Mint Delight

2 8-ounce tubs whipped cream cheese
1 large box banana instant pudding
1 chocolate graham cracker crust
1 small box chocolate-covered mint cookies
2 bananas peeled and cut into rounds

In a large mixing bowl, mix cream cheese until light and fluffy.

Make pudding according to package directions.

Fold together cream cheese, pudding, and bananas.

Place mint cookies in crust to cover bottom and sides.

Spoon in filling.

Chill about 3 hours.

Cut and serve.

Top with whipped topping if desired.

LEVEL OF DIFFICULTY

Justin's Trademark Mini-Cheesecakes

3 tubs whipped Philadelphia cream cheese

3 eggs

1/2 cup sugar

1 teaspoon vanilla extract

1 heaping tablespoon flour

1 box Vanilla Wafers

1 can cherry or blueberry pie filling

mini paper cups

Mix all ingredients, except wafers and pie fillings, in blender.

Place paper cups in a muffin tin.

Place 1 Vanilla Wafer into each paper cup.

Scoop mixture from blender onto top of wafer (fill about halfway—they rise).

Bake at 350 degrees for 20 minutes.

Cool and top with pie filling.

This is my favorite recipe to make.

LEVEL OF DIFFICULTY

Angel's Heavenly Strawberries

1 whole angel food cake
5 cups strawberries, sliced thin
1 tub whipped topping, thawed

Set aside some strawberries to place on top of the cake.

Cut cake horizontally into 3 layers.

Combine 1/2 of the strawberries and 1 1/2 cups whipped topping into a large bowl.

Spread half of the strawberry mixture on cake layer.

Repeat layers, ending with cake.

Frost top and sides of cake with remaining whipped topping.

Place strawberries on top of cake.

Refrigerate at least an hour before serving.

Refrigerate any remaining cake.

Makes 12 servings.

LEVEL OF DIFFICULTY

Santa Claus at the North Pole

1 large box gelatin (cherry or strawberry)

1 8-ounce tub Cool Whip

1 box Christmas-type cookies with red and green sparkles

1 package of pink and green marshmallows

6 mint candy canes

Prepare Jell-O according to package directions.

Place in refrigerator to gel completely.

When done, spread Cool Whip on top and decorate.

I like to use my imagination and build a sidewalk with the marshmallows. All you kids have fun and go for it!

LEVEL OF DIFFICULTY

Nicki's Neato Necklace

4 30-inch pieces shoestring licorice
1 cup fruit-flavored round cereal
$3/4$ cup round bran cereal
$1/2$ cup round toasted oat cereal
$11/2$ rolls Life Savers

Tie a knot at one end of licorice.

Place ingredients into separate bowls.

Make your own necklace by threading cereal and candy onto licorice. Tie knot at other end.

To wear necklace, tie ends together with a double knot.

LEVEL OF DIFFICULTY

Marky's Mice
(Banana Mice)

1 medium banana
lemon juice
sliced almonds
few chocolate chips and a few raisins
1 piece raw spaghetti

Cut banana in half (width).

Brush with lemon juice lightly, let dry.

Press 2 almond slices into top of banana to make ears.

Press 2 raisins to make eyes.

Chocolate chip for nose.

Break spaghetti into 6 small pieces.

Push in around nose to make whiskers.

Makes 2.

KNOCK, KNOCK!

Who's there?
Banana.
Banana who?
Knock knock
Who's there?
Banana.
Banana who?
Knock knock.
Who's there?
Orange.
Orange who?
Orange you glad I didn't say banana?

LEVEL OF DIFFICULTY

127

Casey's Caged Creatures

#1 The Creature
1 banana cut into 1¹/₂-inch pieces

Spread cream cheese or peanut butter on banana piece.
Roll in shredded carrot.
Press in 2 raisins for eyes.
Cut a piece of shoestring licorice for mouth.

#2 The Cage
1 large orange with ends cut off

Cut rest of orange into ¹/₂-inch-thick slices.
Use spinach leaves or parsley to cover on slice of orange
Place on plate.
Place creature in the middle.
Poke wooden or plastic toothpicks into edges of orange slice to make cage bars.
Place another orange slice on top to make roof.

LEVEL OF DIFFICULTY

Justin's Jurassic Dessert

1 16-ounce package chocolate sandwich cookies

2 cups cold milk

1 box chocolate instant pudding

1 8-ounce tub whipped topping

1 package gummy dinosaur candies

8 7-ounce plastic cups

Crush package of cookies in sandwich bags. To do this, place cookies in bag, close bag, and beat with a rolling pin.

Pour instant pudding into a large bowl and add 2 cups of cold milk.

Stir in whipped topping and add half of the crushed cookies.

Stir for 2 minutes with a whisk.

Let mixture stand for 5 minutes.

Place 3 tablespoons of crushed cookies into bottom of each plastic cup.

Add instant pudding mixture until cup is three-quarters full.

Sprinkle some of the remaining crushed cookies on top for dirt effect.

Place cups in refrigerator for 1 hour.

Place dinosaurs on top and serve.

LEVEL OF DIFFICULTY

Chef Justin Miller lives with his mom and dad in Pennsylvania. This is his first book.

For more information on Justin Miller, please write:

Chef Justin Fan Club

P.O. Box 94

Baden, PA 15005

Index

Index

Metric Conversion Tables

WEIGHTS

Ounces and Pounds	Metrics
$1/4$ ounce	7 grams
$1/3$ ounce	10 g
$1/2$ ounce	14 g
1 ounce	28 g
1 $1/3$ ounces	42 g
1 $3/4$ ounces	50 g
2 ounces	57 g
3 ounces	85 g
3 $1/2$ ounces	100 g
4 ounces ($1/4$ pound)	114 g
6 ounces ±	70 g
8 ounces ($1/2$ pound)	227 g
9 ounces	250 g
16 ounces (1 pound)	464 g

LIQUID MEASURES

tsp.=teaspoon   Tbs.=tablespoon

Spoons and Cups	Metrics
$1/4$ tsp.	1.23 milliliters
$1/2$ tsp.	2.5 mm
$3/4$ tsp.	3.7 mm
1 tsp.	5 mm
1 desert spoon	10 mm
1 Tbs.(3 tsp.)	15 mm
2 Tbs. (1 ounce)	30 mm
$1/4$ cup	60 mm
$1/3$ cup	80 mm
$1/2$ cup	120 mm
$2/3$ cup	160 mm
$3/4$ cup	180 mm
1 cup	240 mm
2 cups (1 pint)	480 mm
3 cups	720 mm
4 cups (1 quart)	± liter
4 quarts (1 gallon)	3 $3/4$ liters

TEMPERATURES

°F (Fahrenheit)	°C (Centigrade or Celcius)
32 (water freezes)	0
200	95
212 (water boils)	100
250	120
275	135
300 (slow oven)	150
325	160
350 (moderate oven)	175
375	190
400 (hot oven)	205
425	220
450 (very hot oven)	232
475	245
500 (extremely hot oven)	260

LENGTH

U.S. Measurements	Metrics
$1/8$ inch	3 mm
$1/4$ inch	6 mm
$3/8$ inch	1 cm
$1/2$ inch	1.2 cm
$3/4$ inch	2 cm
1 inch	2.5 cm
1 $1/4$ inches	3.1 cm
1 $1/2$ inches	3.7 cm
2 inches	5 cm
3 inches	7.5 cm
4 inches	10 cm
5 inches	12.5 cm

APPROXIMATE EQUIVALENTS

1 kilo is slightly more than 2 pounds

1 liter is slightly more than 1 quart

1 meter is slightly more than 3 feet

1 centimeter is approximately $3/4$ inch